Barn Burned, Then

Winner of the
2008 Omnidawn Poetry Prize
selected by
Marjorie Welish

Barn Burned, Then

Michelle Taransky

OMNIDAWN PUBLISHING
RICHMOND, CALIFORNIA
2009

Cover art by Richard Taransky
Leading Man Falling Into
Charcoal and pastel on paper, 24 x 36 inches
Copyright © Richard Taransky 2009

Book cover and interior design by Ken Keegan

Offset printed in the United States on archival, acid-free recycled paper
by Thomson-Shore, Inc., Dexter, Michigan

Omnidawn Publishing is committed to preserving ancient
forests and natural resources. We elected to print this title on
30% postconsumer recycled paper, processed chlorine-free. As
a result, for this printing, we have saved:

1 Trees (40' tall and 6-8" diameter)
594 Gallons of Wastewater
1 million BTUs of Total Energy
36 Pounds of Solid Waste
123 Pounds of Greenhouse Gases

Omnidawn Publishing made this paper choice because our
printer, Thomson-Shore, Inc., is a member of Green Press
Initiative, a nonprofit program dedicated to supporting authors,
publishers, and suppliers in their efforts to reduce their use of
fiber obtained from endangered forests.

For more information, visit www.greenpressinitiative.org

Environmental impact estimates were made using the Environmental Defense
Paper Calculator. For more information visit: www.edf.org/papercalculator

Library of Congress Catalog-in-Publication Data

Taransky, Michelle.
    Barn burned, then / Michelle Sarah Taransky.
       p. cm.
    ISBN 978-1-890650-43-8 (pbk. : alk. paper)
    I. Title.
    PS3620.A7289B37 2009
    811'.6--dc22

                                                        2009030675

Published by Omnidawn Publishing, Richmond, California
www.omnidawn.com   (510) 237-5472   (800) 792-4957

            10 9 8 7 6 5 4 3 2 1

            ISBN: 978-1-890650-43-8

ACKNOWLEDGEMENTS

Thank you to the editors of the following publications, where some of these poems originally appeared: *88, The Continental Review, Court Green, Denver Quarterly, GlitterPony, La Petite Zine, Little Red Leaves, New American Writing, notnostrums, Parcel, Thermos* and *The City Visible: Chicago Poetry for the New Century* (Cracked Slab 2007). "The Bank Holds" was first published under a different title in a chapbook, *The Plans Caution* (QUEUE 2007).

Writing these poems was made possible, in part, by a residency at the Wave Books Poetry Farm. Many thanks to Lisa, Rick, Henry, James, Pearl and Brian for showing me the farm life.

I am indebted to the continued guidance and support of my generous teachers and friends: Dan Beachy-Quick, Meg Barboza, Ava Dellaira, Robert Hass, Oren Izenberg, Ben Kopel, Dee Morris, Caryl Pagel, Emily Pettit, Srikanth Reddy, Matthias Regan, Jordan Stempleman, and Karen Volkman. Thank you for showing me what poetry can do. To Marjorie Welish, Rusty Morrison and Ken Keegan, my total gratitude.

Finally, I could not imagine having written this book without the love of my parents, Richard and Elizabeth Taransky, and Petey.

CONTENTS

for my parents:

BURN BOOK

I seem to know what I mean to do, and seem to be myself; I would like to get the thing said, I would like rather to get it thought, to grasp it—I look at things and they become large, like barns, I feel lost and yet they are not big enough—merely a little clumsy, reminiscent and clumsy.

—George Oppen

I care about poetry that disrupts business as usual.

—Charles Bernstein

Barn Burning, That

Empty will take care
Ask, can our digging
Do the job, untell
What crier told

Only stories grow tall
No fossil wrote in
Wasn't the emblem of the whale
Ordered from confession to cave

That stores names

That had to be fed to the children

Barn, you turned away at that
Lip— decreed ballads not
Knowing the country planted itself

Felt bones in the way
We stood for

Frontiersmen meaning it
Object over hero, cry
Whiteness and mantis may
Be white, proceed I am
Burning the portrait
That barn painted over the dig

The barn will pose
Or translation hasn't helped
Pile yes with no that stall
Means we farm moths as well
As the chapter in chapter

Using the same procedures
Pound headless cattle
Cage in the open field

How To Keep
Your Balance
On A

Galloping horse. Don't try galloping

The first time

You are punctuating

Correctly. My butcher promised

A picture of a three-hearted goat with

The picture crossed

Out. Silhouette of a baby.

She was a revised instruction set

A mother and the sorry I

Of the picture. The picture snuffing out

Before it caught you

Were looking at the moral. Its glass that cut

The cow's tongue. Because of having

Said forever and then

Romance. In the middle of this

Job. I was

Telling a little story

Sewing the split

Eye back while the dog is

At eight different doors.

Declare library. Lie concerning

Date of union. My butcher

Refuses to number

The shop. And stole. Did she mean map?

Followed the un-

Folding butcher

Butchering for the town's

Shank bone. They resemble a haul

When it is about winning. Cover the church.

Eat the kid in his mother's milk. The last

Picture of the latest babies

Named after storms

The plots they fall on

Are falling on

Barn Burner, If

What lies down here
Does not call for
The plan

Its facts of carve
And split something
Rare to hillocks like

The frock
Wants the unwed
Story of fault

A place to
Hold fawns if
Slatted if elder spare the

Full of body for
A final spot
In the clearing only

If it wasn't bough
But corner of petite
Angle the leave's

Curling margins
If ovate
Then

. . .   Blaze the
Bricks will

I don't stop for

Then the yearling
Loses touch

18

Barn Burning, It

Found ways for following
Tempest like first ground

Breaking idea of foundation

First till a mule

Because disasters care
For if, asking is no bulwark

That one thought brick but
Breathe it states that missing

Patch of claim flowers

While planting burn
Not the burning

Reason ash is
Saved will figure

As such reconciliation
Tends to waste

Light: it falls in

What interest in fire-
Fed prizes

Calf and their comparisons

State's birds called
Northern flicker,
Barn swallow

A charm to quiet bundles

Owing a companion

First meadow that alit

Then no plume
Can be its flint

Barn Burner, A Call

He owns the field

Memorial for conviction
Place where split beckons

Between stage and the stag
An unsharpened knife used

In house making church

I said it's from the lost chapter

And an invention— delusion of caw
Asking yes saying label

Siren from segment
From departing

Fence of breathing
Salute of sharecrop

Minion had been used
Was scansion

As I was told

The same place will
Father idea, stand for the
Stanza— a house

Where replacement flowers
Invention is numbered
Temple, the scare,
Third moment about courage teacher

Difference between red and bird is
One is red

Barn Burner, An Epitaph

I lie

the plans with no lathe
set them timbers down leveled their ends
a hex the scale of peasant fancy

for a neighborhood girl, does the infinite
remain? have you already drawn the curtains
found the dining room set you're leaving for

if the war
starts, which side
will we join

Barn Burning, An Eclogue

For those who say it is enough
Of the farmstead, not falling

Rain come last to bed and tearing
White sheets into small armies of animals

Where this keeper's concern meets
Old thrasher in the shed

Its keyhole patterned
After a breast and the calling

A lake we had built
Filled with response

A response then

Respond, respond with a weed to
The flames stopped to

Track a doe

I don't know how
Barn is like grave

Matter and matters
Like a silo missing its torso the
Barn's reading rooms

Forgetting-weeds mirror what
Was kept in the safe, same as others
Have divorced a few apple trees with no ideas

About red
As if it has two mother

Languages— they are the bad pruners
The unhorse
Crediting the no

Barn Burner, I

Glinted with fever
Greeting stable-eyes
How it was before

The barn—In dreams
Who is to say a ravine
Say forlorn had not

Lain crop—There were
Fevers to greet a narrator

With three farm names
It was before a choke

On ashen errors of weeds
Or else splinters himself

Inside the lost barn
Locked and round how

It was burning
Dreaming the asking
What first match
Took from dowry

Wood stop breathing burn
Warning shepherd about shelter

The shift from somewhere as this
Guttering the lamp had made
No dream where hexes were

A paper fruit or felled woods
Dew that would not sublime—Spark

In the steeple
Bard didn't spark
Mother
Country put it this way
We have to talk

Barn Burning

If I'd frown. Hide
from. The dog
wood stains. If wide
farm I'd place, hold
her dog. Would fawn
if trees. If older. Wood

rings. Like a slate
scraped. I'd wash
old skin. Clean
again, do fold
down the corner. Silos
are piles raking up

the scattered dew
covered leaves. If
the shades are already drawn,
find the barn. Over
turned. Broken
into sap, bark and shake.

Barn Burner, Say It

The grubber said from what the notes
Said he had fallen on too

Many occasions last fall
Yes the fault of roots

A crooked walk or borrowed
Bones not due to taking care

Of our ailing want
To piece back together

All that has parted

Barn from us
And they

Wanted walls in place
Of the worrying

Plot's position and our
Unproven theories for building

A building at the fault
Line and mistaking that

Winter remains
A visible cause said

For the wailing that concerns
Math's forecast and what is owed

To the early snow
That is covering the barn

That doesn't mean

It's not there

In the last stages of the same disease

Each of us in need of the figure
From the past in case there's no one

Who cares where
Your temper came from
It' s been good for the plan, this
The first farmer to outlive his barn

Instead of taking pictures he is where
Waiting at the door

A Promise Is

To promise I haven't spent

Any

  —Time wandering

At sea— I know this farm is

Our craft

Bank Barn

The barn built into the land is a small child
Speaking for the cattle's tracks
Like a bride this window grazes
It's beautiful, not lucky
A buyer who doesn't need
To check a harvest before
Trading— Not even a mountain
Could have a barn like this
A view of everyone
Else's spotted horses
Drinking oceans
What about them
Can't be followed

A Flower Within

A flower within a flower whose history
Pressed paradox

At an idea of the particular harvest— One volume
As a relief, as thirteen different voices

Those hard takes
By mast
You blame the mast
The entrances like seraphs
Are exiting and are
The falling for another
River called Parent
The parents said no no we are not going
To cross

It's is not a ghost in their desert
Ghost not ghetto but what was
Got in the word the ghost had

Left and let a war cry
Without a word to cross

First shot where
We were crossed they
Are not diseases they are a mistake being made

A shot—   Shorter description of the building

Depending on
Who forfeits it
And saluted all
The inviolate
Working to place

Glory by hold
Old lead-salute

As though uproar not
Flying firm it
Affirmed: bulwark
You are howling

That lasts
And yes that
Waits in the kindling
Of addresses

Evading horse-traders as both
Trader and horse are flittering

Great falls

Habit from boxcar
Boxcar gilded or fallen apart
At the silken bank notes
Should halyard move the farmstead's
Fictive flag-poles

Repetition pulses
The key to key
Open a lock
To get

Well and to be
Bringing a spark

Time seized the eyelid
Oldest dream about
Twitch and creak
That I made the sixth book
Burn

Made a machine and then a machine
To burn the machine
Machine
Exist patriot exists despite being
Forgotten through a window

Building a camera
To title it

In the follower's resting-
Place between black
Is blind as grubber's orders

For The Ends of Barns, And

for any cutting
mechanism or warm
machine that will

keep on
counting the lost
is or dead plot

has come to
look like
the cause

that forced crying
calves away from
their mothers

who are torn
are errors
we bring tamed

to the teller
as she says no
act is misplaced in them

our window's bullet holes
where the shooting is still

heard because the barn

swallow and the bank swallow are
here and here won't

keep no one
apart from the sight

Preface

No you haven't seen
pictures. No you never were born
in the barn. Yes
we will go to the
no it is not a story. Here
the sentence needs
to be completed. It was the sentence
the detective decided
the robber
deserved.

BANK BOOK

They sold the calf. That fall the bank took over

—Genevieve Taggard

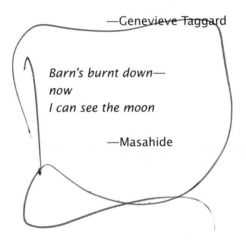

*Barn's burnt down—
now
I can see the moon*

—Masahide

Barn Burned, Then

The bank,
A teller,
The same figures'

Capacity to chorus, as if
Light was beaten for bread

A confessed wage
Through another

Chance-flood

Broken-necked flicker

Gold pawed labyrinth

Flints of past thresher

Taking brother who is best
At hiding

Writing a statement

To take the barn's place

What Is Counted

The land changed hands the warning stayed the same

Like looking is the arm is debt. Not flame

Or risk-owl power for widening, when there

Is a fallen out illustration of turn

That used no fence. No ash-tree to blame.

Value ran with our herd saying myself

I meant it gone. Name spoiled a name. Fire has

Planted over lifeblood again and called out to

Stay put your coat down eat a bit of this

Stolen idea of worth. Wait for the change

To learn what's been counted, turned into feed.

Our collected sightings are not yours. You say I am scared

Of intent. The possibility of a barn for animals

You forgot to tame. A boundary stone is moving

By its own will. Because the rooster crows

It was trauma. Was crowing like a habit

And the difficulty of yelling just a part

To the burglar, to the banker taking your error

Into the vault. Returning to howl *we're through*

The book, a ledger of turnover asking matter

Not to influence the liar. You are past

The past at odds with his landworker.

So it sounds just like everyone is saying

Burn the storm-door in a war. I had

Started to say I'm sorry, and then

The decay of nevertheless. The tense

Showing a not breathing crop. A picker

Of bruised fruit is being

Introduced. Is inciting an excuse

No confession can

Account for

This change.

They Sold The Calf. That Fall

The bank took over. What had been
the farm. The particular

that is described in entry 8. By that year
he was a member. Planning hearings,

writing: museums are translations of field
activities. Letters in response to letters

from architects in alphabetical sequence from
"abaca" to "zinnia." Paid to the family. To raise

native grasses, forests, and appropriate means
for measure. Boundaries should be

inspected. General views included. And the originals,
taken by farmers, working closely with duststorms, shelter,

emergencies arranged in the National Portrait Gallery
by year. By which progress could be the work of the weather

that is labeled "Domestic," indexed by name of the live-
stock responsible for making sugar from cornstalks.

Wild flowers are not documented. In the diseases of the general
the construction is not to be confused with the center, copies of loans

sent after this March are missing. Droughts vary in content. Crops
matter. Each disturbance is responsible. A farmer bearing

his name. On the farm radio program
was the farm. Responsible for planting fall

crops distributed as places. Estimating a fever
to show the extent of the overprinted threats. To form

the plan for breeding grounds. In the home
the home was slaughtered, was divided in two parts:

an experimental laboratory and a speech
made daily. The chronological copies of breakdowns. It describes

many bodies
carried on. This is almost an act. A photograph of prisoners

of war picking peaches.

Building The Bank, Asking

Who called the bank

The bank of

Grave the bank

You asked for praying

Mantis

When she handed us the bill her hands were
Hands of a farmhand

It's good to have the image in mind.
At the bank.
Farmed stoppages
Selling a model townscape
Confrontation of milk and made
Never less resistance
To read the entire deed at once
Left for the vultures
Crime seen by one-
Eyed barn owl I caught
To keep the farmscene
Unlike a name
Changing to tender

A Stutter, Following

A stutter, number after number, apologies, the resemblance of the forest

To the axe's handle, one tree, how many lions can be carved from it,

Whose hand you held at the investigation, the funeral, the dedication, as

Evidence is placed in a glass case to be considered, see the sorry teller

Counting change, a crime and a crisis recounted in the same breaths,

Bird eating bird bones, the will to witness what you have been

Saving up, a robber behaving like a fallen fence, two streams that go

By one name, a condition developed in turn, in chorus with the crying

Hoarded eggshells that will rot, no matter how long, they spelled this

May change, into ways you consider it, which is to say, how not to feel

Broken, wings are the sum, and counting, and counting the present

State, a disaster is, waiting to happen, because the pile was made up,

Of branches not yet dead, and you refusing, to say tinder,

To admit, potential for tender, there, I said it, said please

Ask who is about to tell, the particular was impossible,

To keep up, doing this, and this to our hiding place

Great Foundation I Dug Out

to place

a once

dead barn swallow—

        now full of change

        and falling

it is an anvil

stuffed with wild

weeds I saved to open up

an account

an account for holding

spoken of

as well as since then not mentioned

this as a real
important sound that is
the sound to carry
crossing of the roots

the matter in the
verbena and cash
crop, too. flowers I picked
on the way to the
falling walls

Bank Branch

State of fall
I mean fall
Leaves

Saying a season
Is not an only answer

Probability of rotting
That permits

Door-keeper as well
As the door he left

A teller never their
Worries about

The red horse &
Confession
Folded into threshold

Glass statement
Promising I won't see you anymore
A likeness

Here fixing causes that dream
To be about a bank

A blood-like retreat
From root
For trust

Going to war

Changing brother is

Going to get there

Bank Run

Withdraw

As a bird call: *barn burner*
You made the bank take place

Paint over gleaner
Over reaper whose craft was
Rows, a gap, security

Like banking on
Death sentences
The architect's unbuilt work

Teller has no reason
In such a
State of firebricks

Safe for ember
& bad currencies
Are safes for ivory
For winter

Spelling themselves

An image with breath
How say saved

Testament, kept it in place
Of the letter of credit

& signed it with the family

Name like a fallen flicker

Safe because of the safe

Teller's Poem

Is a cave
A cause
Coming
For a confession

How did the farm go?
On like a particular
What season is this?
An overturned tree means bad luck
So, manor are you fasting?
I'm a soundling—no
Manor do you know lovebirds?
I've got habits

Spell *the clearing took up*

What's the banker to do?
Collect, cry, sleep
Where?
Into the plain

How tend to fire?
Like
A ritual tree
A carving for goldness
A craft can't help

Bank in the cellar
Scared of turning
Signs like a closed keyhole
Did sound like sad rooms
With quiet characters

You left like a ladder
My robber with no memory

Of flickers' cares
Memorial plot of forgetting-plants
A weed that counters

For Telling

A hoarse voice is to fail
Careful start of a howl

History of divided holdings
Unsaid witness to half-lives

Masked trust— A made bed it
Proceeds from the fold like

The third oldest view of plague
Then pretty-faced timeline

My guided parade   Come observer
As if the heart-shaped would

Confess backwards gleams
Find promise not a traitor

Ballad

When burglar yelled our lie at noon
"No herd will be your gold"— The bank had
Run the barn a toy of wood

The teller dreamed
A horse with a silk chimney
Instructions for the quiet:

A safe won't
Burn— it stands, it calls,
You're bound to
Buy

And then a fever from black corn,
Favorite crop

Turned into an escape
Craft— What
is working is the barn owl bought

To imitate that thing's call
We do not count

The curse's harm
Or ask for fields
To plough

The banker, like the burglar
When burned
Forget our vow

Fall Instructions

In the safe you will

Find the combination to open the fire safe

At the end of the world

Is an argument and its stolen

Negotiator putting stones

Into the wild

Fire

Into saying wills will want to forgive

You and change you who made matter

And measured night falling on

That space that is afforded them

Did them put them in a ditch

Burying them and buried their ashes if

Then there

The smoke clouds are burglars

Are all we know is that it is the fall

So far we had come so far

Along the edge worrying about impending

Falls into the line of grave the graves'

Diggers are crying

Wolf where there is no need

For accounting the mistaking

Of the property lines for babies

I cannot help

Myself but cry whenever anyone else is

Crying

Is placing all

The firewood in the firesafe

We will make sure we storm

Out before the fall

When we are told to count

Casualties I asked you to keep time

That time it would have been enough to be-

Fall us

The Way The Bank Works

Is by fire— the turning brings it
Back from its
Gallows bird's cage

The keep from where
This line came at I is the way
The bank will

Limit whatnot to less cries
In these times adders
Can be a storm mustering

To mask an approach
Robber has a plan

Arrive before five marks
And if there is aftermath

Reference the one who arrived
Then arrived late at last

Name. Him in his tongue

Don't say it's a fragment because
The teller is listening
For orders

Put your trust in scraps, in the bank
Notes you are not supposed to remember

A soldier as a dream
About

This is the one where the teller meets the robber
And rations, says it is time
That the adding machine
Fires a mother

To provide a leg for framing
What kind of sentences apply

To that not-sighted banker

Who made a sound like this

The Event

I had over-anticipated the event. I don't understand this idea of construction

Where the cross section of figure, plain, and bondstone are one, four

And seven barns respectively. A crying falcon. You were the one

Who told me girder. Cast the anchor in rich earth. Declaration of echo is no

Different from the fold. When weeds push at the walls, the wailing

Names names

Places

A mirror on the burnt-out

Coop to dare the thunder. Thunder. Our good shovel keeps

Behind glass. We name crimes. Dig up collapsed wings. What

Spade may wander into the safe? Does not break branches

That were once being written. A barn equal to stable

Echoes. The wrong drought to begin the stakes. We can't identify

The woods in our home from fears. Blood-horses. Brave holding

A book about this. A half-step before the calf's step. Take in the falcon

Calling from the farm in flames for more than

A season

A last fall

To spend

The Bank Holds

rapid labor:
9 places in the world to hide:
even exchanging:
cut the land or open it up:
leaps:
rain, reining:
trow song after trow song:
I'd rather not:
buried section:
working a way out:
contract[s]:
saw in the door frame:
is spoken for:
the war's over:
odes for addition:
our people:
depths, abyss, as a well:
they are dreaming:
putting it out:

This is the beggar's way of speaking.

This is the way I've been
Speaking.

The windrows then stolen, are a large gem.
Wanting to watch the brick building
Constantly.

Adding Up The Columns, It's Like

Like thinking of that bank

As a shipwrecking

Mutter stopped at varnish

When it isn't. Another poor

Teller hiding in its doorframe

Counting grains. A bird's

Eye maple you turned into

The pillars.

Think about the number of us who think

We ate a part of a single grand

Champion steer. How it's

Sound is changing overseas.

You believe destruction

Is seen as an eye-scar

When you could say *Let the sum total*

Rings be

Taken to

Drown. The teller has said that

Copying the county's

Bank murals to firing range size

Must work. Master mistiming

It—   His revolver

Painted to look like marble

That started the trust, or

Keeps blackbirds between

The mattress. Muster the

Cross-

Eyed in line with

The crossed.

Revenge

Is the robber's bride

Tied to tropes & clawing for

Jade when you've been told this could

Only be about a woodland.

Standing In The Door, Calling That

the account is present   taking notes   footing where a

footnote struck with lighting   it could have been   done at the hand   the striking

that came back   was a movement   drawn in   circulation   being absent then

then an address   to convert,   fit,   force,   hold,   have,   having been

aggravated   and   so   add   up   to   a   movement

demand an entry   enter with an intent   to scare   the or

your demand for   statement   saving   performing   from   within

the crowd   a swearing that   that safe

held a number of molds   the ledger   tells us this   will

call the danger   the not yet   robbed   past a pasture   a year made

change   how   to   sit   for   the   sermon

a room for all   believers   in only one   house

to   give   it   the   only   name   I   had   for   it

stranger,   stranger,   stranger

Saving For A Purpose

not to talk in defense

of the plain, I could have

bore the charge to

place in the safe folds and ill

flocks of flickers

and if it storms

here then the way to carry

me will change— it's

the dominant patterns of the

barnstorming that dropped handbills

announcing a theft announcing when you

find it it will start again

without knowing how to fence in

was how we weather permitting

measured a barn

a windowless address

put up to the shadow-maker

because you said you

wanted to hold the shape we were in

as possible as a future

pattern for covering the bank's

savings— and for saving, as we had

trouble taking place

Banking Rules

With the entire floor to oneself
It is a sound that stands in for loneliness

Is loneliness, a suspect
I suspect

Summary without currency or
A care to commit to
Crimes of care

Against a figure we cannot
Figure out division
In the first place

I want you to quit
Worrying, the could haves

Meant everything

Bank Note

I haven't figured out what

Way to say the accountable

Parts out loud

It must always remain

More than we

Willed to spend it

In notes—   Notes keep
Losing their
Value while my

Lies carry
Along the vaulted
Ceilings we are telling you to wait to

Bury last year—   To liken the golden
Winged lions
Guarding the key to the safe where

We can't help
But dream that barn is needed to be
These days in need of

Help, all wilderness and forest are
Made from metal
Available for purchase

64

For a spell for will only
The will to balance
A regret
Like a claim
Working against
What happens when they all come to pay

Close attention to today since
Today there is the collecting
Water that falls from the cracks in the

Ceiling at its dividing line
Besides the praying
Mantis who holds me, counts me

As a part of the falling
Drops because there is no more tender
And in all of the credit she is owed

What is on the line
At stake in that note to the teller
Telling me to take the charge to place

Now in the burning plain
Now an illogical marriage
Proposal and a miscarried

Agenda I will and will point to
To not count
The miscarriage's said

Profit & Loss Statement

I have been a gypsy a couple
Of times she said if I said
In the past, each color stood

To remind you your birth
Name was Fox and please quit

Forgetting the charge to hand
Me nothing
But letters

Because they are lies if
Nothing else nothing past tense
Part her wilderness sound

Asleep dreaming the accountant is
Saying how can you imagine anything
Incorrectly— Besides what else is there in addition

To naming the dead fox
Robert and referring to him
As Robber, as Giver

Who gives us dreams of his dreams of the fox-fire
Out of which barely one thrush
Emerged still
The leaves turned I

Swore a storm was
On its way however
Without lightning who is able to tell that

The letter had everything to do
With Robber turning to the teller
To tell her he knows

So what if the piles turn into
Guilt after guilt, where no matter
The ways to a way to admit it

This line is about the theft

It is about time

Safes that stay safe

It's My Business

I have made the choice

To choose a particular

Way of operating the business

Dear,

And her heard he

read *thunder returned* her heart

beat returned

but her hen

but her hen

heard the haunt there her

brethren traded need

there a tear at banter

a turn and tender

ended and entered

near the untread near

an err-tree that had a there

there the reader

bred need

and a broken herd

that breather heard.

Theory For Building Where Fault

Lines meet. You continue to hear the same announcements
As I am hearing on the radio. This fall
It is the same war as the last fall before that February
When you first put your trust in my bank. And now
All I want is to tell you is there is still a space for another
Teller. So come back, come be busy here.
The other investors are throwing things at me that mean
That's a bargain, that's not really a bargain.
A way to get more for less. To stock up on the stolen
For the shortage that is always coming again. And again
You are not. I promise to keep safe your jars
While saving up for the new materials to make it matter
Again. Didn't you begin again to see it was an important note
We both marked, left out of the safe because we left
Each other before our old faults.

If You Call The Barn Burner

A thief and see pictures

Of the barn in each of the bank's

Acute corners

Then pass the butter

In the way of the detective

Looking for ways a photograph could

Keep an aging barn through many falls

Barns built with native

Wood I would have saved

The Y beams why wouldn't they

Fit like the barn

Burner's shadow in the shadow

Falling over the plain

That is fighting them

To credit that last

Detective with calling your name

Out from the falling down foundation

Counting is part of your ritual

Cleansing root from change

From can't you see this

Ritual is what keeps you

Alive like the measured wall

Waiting for what has been

Given away to the hiding

Places let go fear

Of staying open

Becoming broke

NOTES

Epigraphs are from *The Selected Letters of George Oppen* edited by
Rachel Blau DuPlessis (Duke 1990), *A Poetics* by Charles Bernstein
(Harvard 1992), *Revolutionary Memory: Recovering the Poetry of the
American Left* by Cary Nelson (Routledge 2003), and *Cage of Fireflies:
Modern Japanese Haiku* edited by Lucien Stryk (Swallow 1993).

"They Sold The Calf. That Fall The Bank Took Over" uses only text
from *Preliminary Inventory of the Records of the Office of the
Secretary of Agriculture : Record Group 16* compiled by Helen
Finneran Ulibarri. (National Archives & Records Service 1979).

"A flower within a flower whose history" is from *Paterson* by William
Carlos Williams (New Directions 1963).

"I had over-anticipated the event. I don't understand this idea of
construction" is from *Frame (1971-1999)* by Barrett Watten (Sun &
Moon 2000).

Michelle Taransky received a BA from the University of Chicago
and an MFA from the Iowa Writers' Workshop. With her father,
architect Richard Taransky, she is the coauthor of the chapbook
The Plans Caution (QUEUE 2007). Her poems have appeared in
Denver Quarterly, VOLT, How2, New American Writing, and other
publications. She currently lives in Philadelphia, where she works at
Kelly Writers House and teaches poetry at Temple University.